I0828203

THIS BOOK BELONGS TO:

WELCOME
TO VIRGINIA

VIRGINIA
SIC SEMPER TYRANNIS

Dedicated to B.F.

ISBN 978-1-958985-86-1

www.joeysavestheday.com

A Mimi Book

Virginia was named in honor of Queen Elizabeth I of England. Early English explorers chose the name to celebrate her. At first, “Virginia” described a huge area along the East Coast, but over time, it became the name of the state we know today.

ENGLAND

VIRGINIA

Virginia is one of the oldest places in the United States. Native American groups lived here long before the English founded Jamestown in 1607, the first permanent English settlement in North America. Virginia played a major role in the American Revolution and became a state in 1788. Many early presidents were born here, and the state was a key location during the Civil War. Today, Virginia is known for its historic sites that help tell the story of America's beginnings.

Virginia was the tenth state to join the Union.
It officially joined on June 25, 1788.

10th

Virginia is located in the Southeastern and Mid-Atlantic region of the United States. It is bordered by Maryland, North Carolina, Tennessee, Kentucky, and West Virginia.

Richmond is the capital of Virginia.
It officially became the capital in 1780.

Richmond, Virginia, has an estimated population of about 233,600 people.

Virginia is the thirty-fifth largest state in the United States by area.

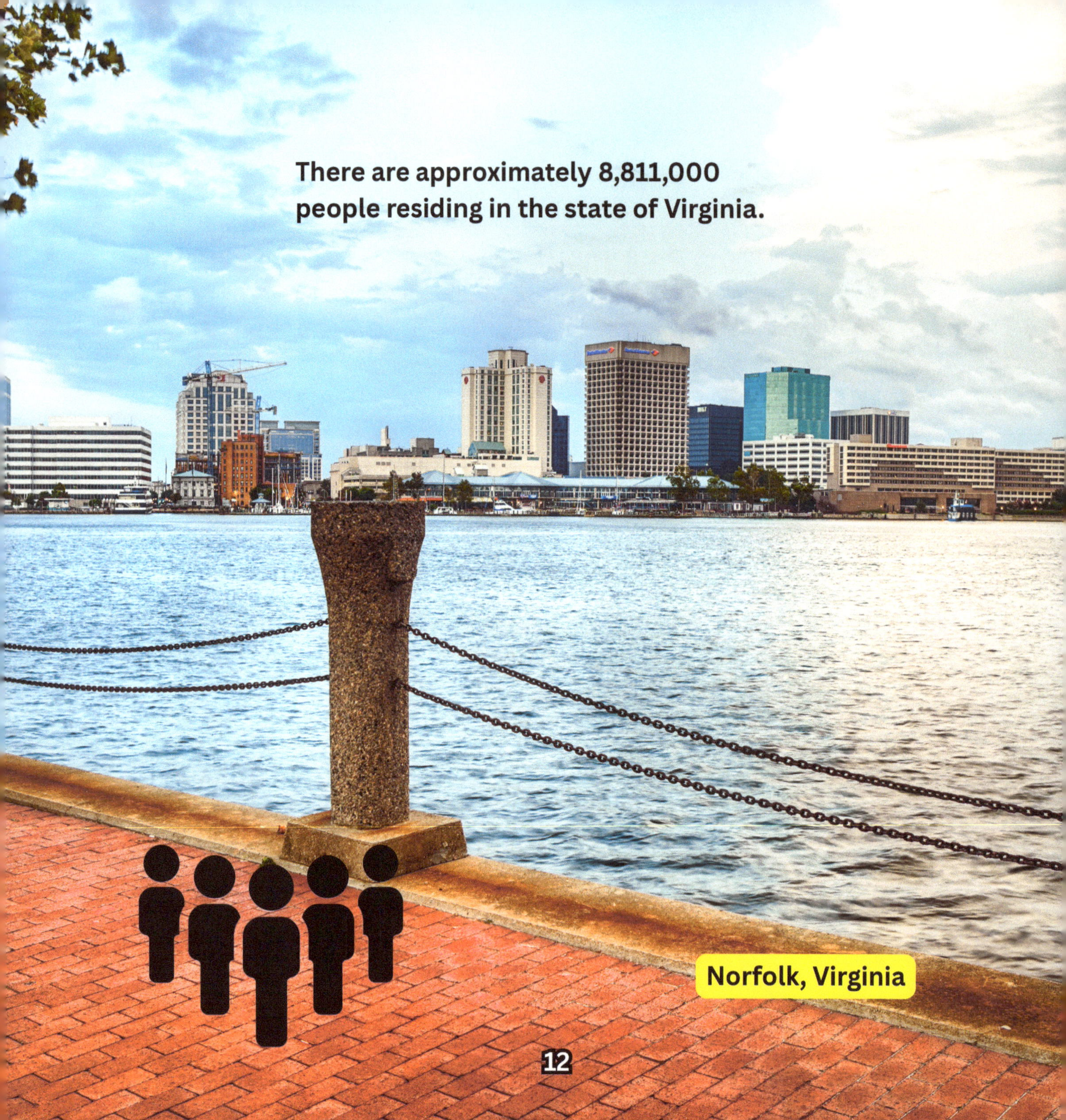

There are approximately 8,811,000 people residing in the state of Virginia.

Norfolk, Virginia

BRAVE

George Washington was born in Westmoreland County, Virginia, and grew up on the banks of the Potomac River. He became a brave leader during the American Revolution and later served as the very first President of the United States.

Virginia is known for its delicious country ham, especially the kind made in the town of Smithfield. This ham is salt-cured and aged, giving it a rich, savory flavor that people have enjoyed for hundreds of years. Families in Virginia often serve it during holidays and celebrations, and it's considered one of the state's most traditional foods.

Virginia

There are 95 counties in Virginia.

Here is a list of twenty of those counties:

Craig	Hanover	Prince Edward	Shenandoah
Dinwiddie	Isle of Wight	Pulaski	Smyth
Fauquier	Mecklenburg	Pittsylvania	Surry
Gloucester	Northampton	Rockingham	Wise
Halifax	Orange	Russell	York

Dark Hollow Falls is one of the most popular waterfalls in Shenandoah National Park, located right off Skyline Drive at milepost 50.7. The trail begins just steps from the road and leads downhill through a cool, shady forest filled with mossy rocks, mountain laurel, and the sound of rushing water. The waterfall tumbles down a series of rocky ledges, creating a sparkling white cascade that kids love to watch up close. Families often stop at the lower viewpoint to feel the mist and enjoy the peaceful forest around them.

The first official Thanksgiving in America didn't take place in Plymouth; it actually happened at Berkeley Plantation, a historic site along the James River in Charles City County. Tucked between Richmond and Williamsburg, this peaceful riverside location is where English settlers gathered in 1619 to give thanks for their safe arrival.

James River

BE THANKFUL BE Grateful & BE BLESSED

The Chesapeake Bay Bridge–Tunnel is one of Virginia's most famous engineering landmarks. It stretches 17.6 miles across the mouth of the Chesapeake Bay and is known for being both a bridge and a tunnel. Opened in 1964, it allows cars to travel over the water and then dive underground so ships can pass safely above. It is considered one of the longest bridge–tunnel systems in the world and is an important connection between mainland Virginia and the Eastern Shore.

The Virginia state bird is the Northern Cardinal. It was chosen as the state bird in 1950.

The official state flower of Virginia is the American Dogwood. It was chosen as the state flower in 1918.

Old Dominion State & Mother of States

A couple of Virginia's nicknames include the Old Dominion State and the Mother of States.

Portsmouth, Virginia

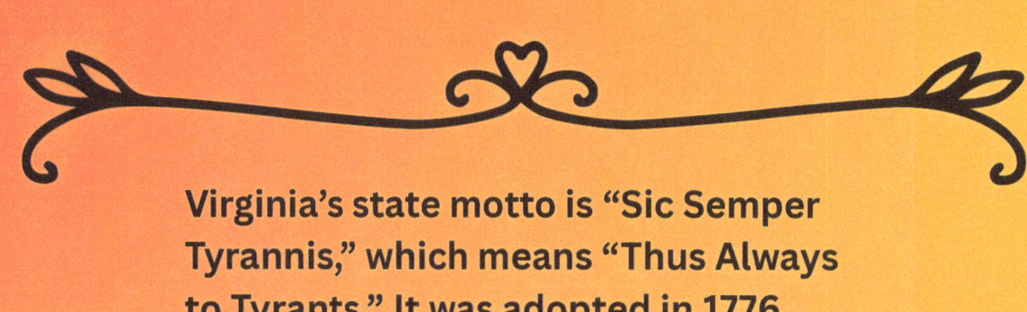

Virginia's state motto is "Sic Semper Tyrannis," which means "Thus Always to Tyrants." It was adopted in 1776.

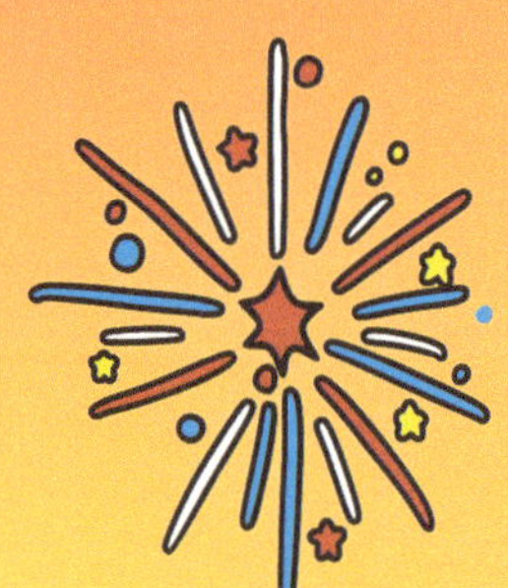
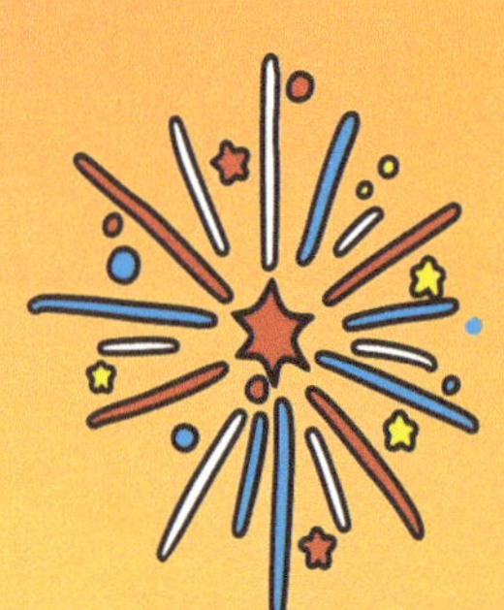

Always

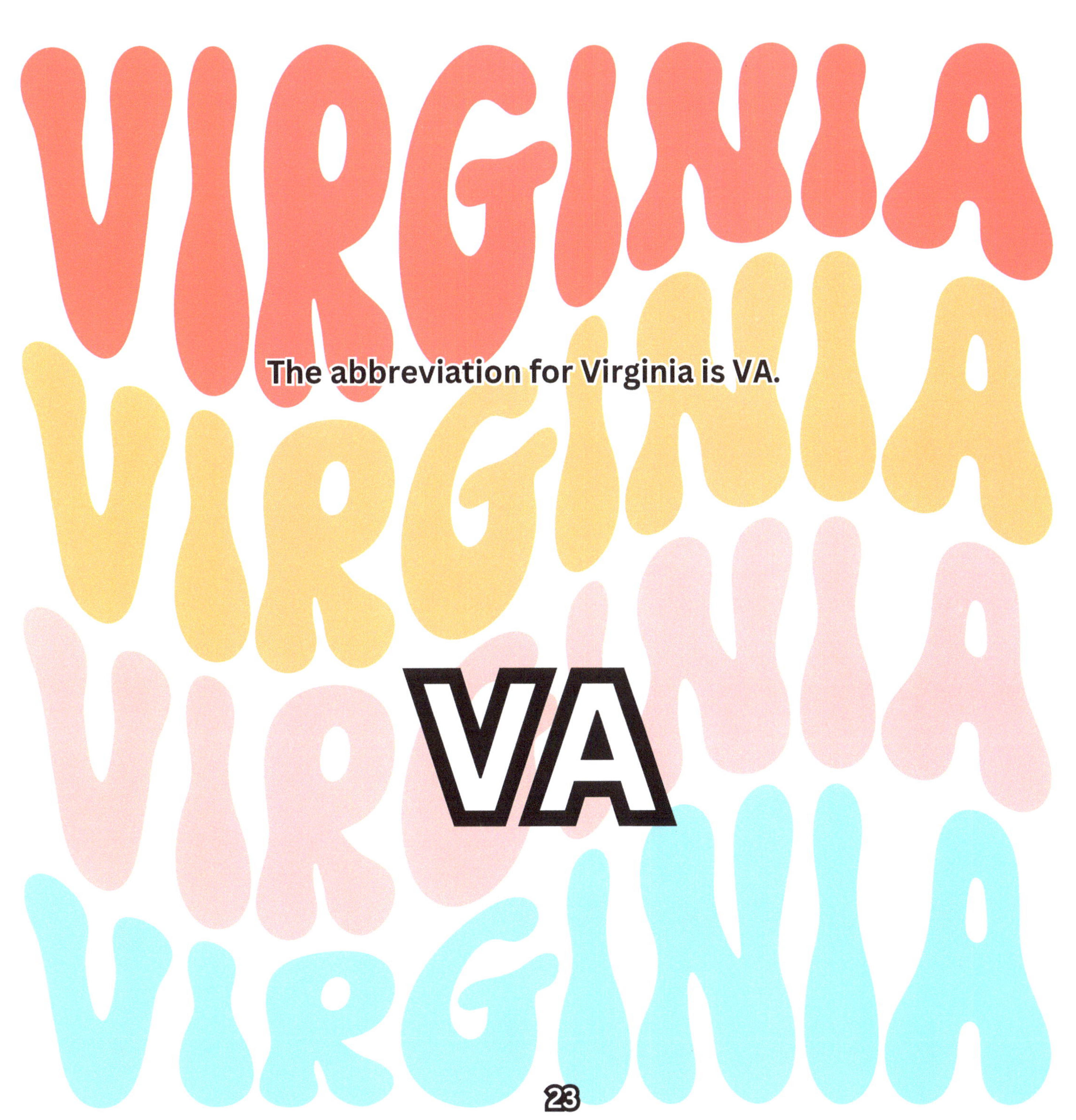

The abbreviation for Virginia is VA.

VA

Virginia's state flag was officially adopted in 1861.

Some crops grown in Virginia are
corn, soybeans, peanuts, and wheat.

Some animals that live in Virginia are white-tailed deer, black bears, red foxes, bobcats, and great horned owls.

Virginia experiences a wide range of temperatures throughout the year. The hottest temperature ever recorded in the state was 110 degrees Fahrenheit, measured in Balcony Falls on July 15, 1954. In contrast, the coldest temperature documented was −30 degrees Fahrenheit, recorded in Pembroke on January 22, 1985.

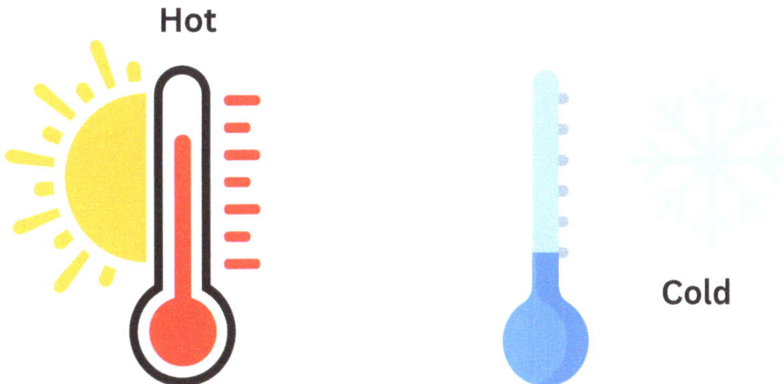

The Virginia Zoo in Norfolk is a wonderful place to explore, with hundreds of animals from around the world. Kids can see lions, elephants, giraffes, red pandas, and playful primates, along with colorful birds and reptiles.

Robert E. Lee was born on January 19, 1807, in Stratford Hall, a historic plantation home in Westmoreland County, Virginia.

The Robert E. Lee Monument once stood in Richmond, Virginia, and for many years it was one of the city's most famous landmarks. It showed a large bronze statue of Robert E. Lee riding his horse, placed high on a tall stone base. Over time, people in Virginia and across the country began talking about what the statue meant and whether it still represented the values of today. After many community conversations, the monument was removed in 2021.

The largest airport in Virginia is Washington Dulles International Airport, located in Dulles, just outside the nation's capital. It sits at 1 Saarinen Circle and serves as the main travel hub for people flying in and out of Virginia. This airport connects travelers to cities all across the country and to destinations around the world, making it one of the busiest and most important airports on the East Coast.

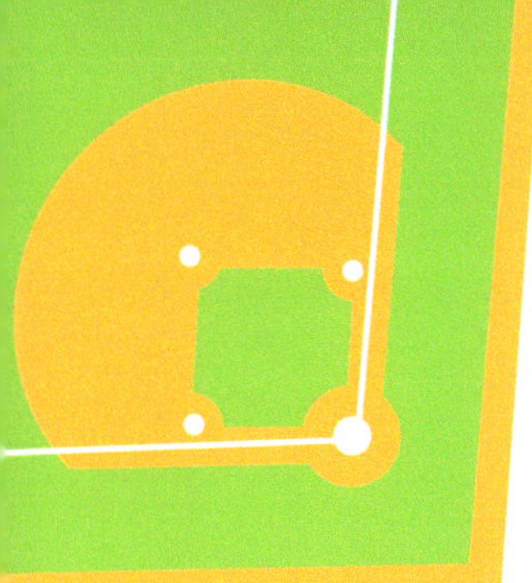

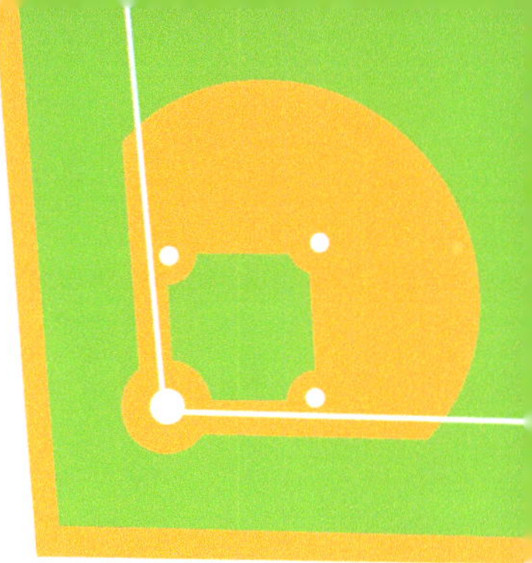

The Richmond Flying Squirrels are a Minor League Baseball team based in Richmond, the capital of Virginia. They play their home games at The Diamond, a bright and lively ballpark known for its fun family atmosphere and playful mascots. The Flying Squirrels are the Double-A affiliate of the San Francisco Giants, which means many future major-league players spend time on this team as they build their skills.

FOOTBALL

The Washington Commanders are a major professional football team with a huge fan base in Virginia, where many families cheer for them every season. The team plays its home games at FedExField in nearby Landover, Maryland, a loud and energetic stadium filled with fans wearing burgundy and gold.

The flowering dogwood is Virginia's state tree. It's known for its soft white or pink blossoms that brighten forests and neighborhoods each spring. The dogwood was officially adopted as the state tree in 1956, and its gentle blooms have become a beloved symbol of Virginia's natural beauty.

The brook trout is Virginia's state fish. It's a small, colorful fish with bright spots and a shimmering pattern that makes it easy to recognize in cool mountain streams. The brook trout was officially adopted as the state fish in 1993, and it's loved for its beauty and its connection to Virginia's clean, flowing waters.

Can you name these?

I hope you enjoyed learning about Virginia.

To explore fun facts about the other 49 states, visit my website at www.joeysavestheday.com. You'll also find a wide variety of homeschool resources to support joyful learning at home. If you enjoyed this book, I would be grateful if you left a review. Your feedback truly helps. Thank you for your support!

Check out these other interesting books in the
50 States Fact Books Series!

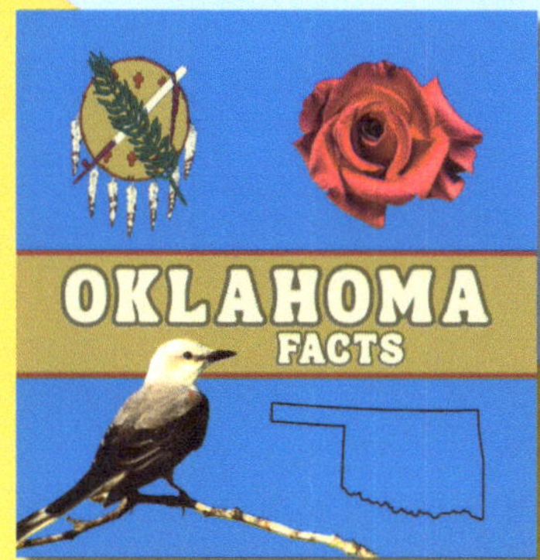

www.mimibooks.com